BETTER TO BE BROKEN

RICK HUNTRESS

Thank you for your love and friendship,

Rick Huntress

Sable Creek
PRESS

Cover and text design by Diane King, dkingdesigner.com

Scripture taken from the King James Version. Public domain.

Published by Sable Creek Press, PO Box 12217, Glendale, Arizona 85318
www.sablecreekpress.com

Library of Congress Control Number: 2012938825

ISBN 978-0-9828875-9-2

Printed in the United States of America.

To Wendy

*Without your support and unconditional love, this
book would certainly never have been written.*

———

To Wendy, Kara, and Ariel

*You have demonstrated your love to me in
a way that reflects how God desires each
of us to love. You are an integral part of
everything that I have accomplished in life.*

———

*A man with faults, to find such love, is truly blessed.
And I am blessed beyond measure.*

CONTENTS

Foreword 7

1 There Has Been an Accident 9

2 Who Am I? 17

3 A Ride to Forget 33

4 The Making of a Man 39

5 Personal Reflection 51

6 Rehabilitation 57

7 Going Home 65

8 911 75

9 The Mighty Hunter 85

10 With Wings as Eagles 91

Appendixes 99

　　We Can Still Dream 109

　　Testimony and Poem by Joyce Folsom Johnson 119

Epilogue 121

FOREWORD

"Before God can use a man greatly, he must first wound him deeply."—A.W. Tozer

*"Great hearts can only be made by great troubles."
—C.H. Spurgeon*

In the common language of the world, a "broken man" is a failure. In fact, the Urban Dictionary offers this sad, stumbling definition, "A person who has constantly accumulated irreputable (sic) damage throughout their (sic) entire life. Damage which cannot be easily repaired if at all. Also someone who has been beaten into submission by life's adversities or has given up on trying to overcome the obstacles." The great tragedy of brokenness is that it is understood so poorly.

By the world's measurement, even the great King David might have been "a broken man," had he not learned from the consequences of his sin, what he wrote in Psalm 51:17, "The sacrifices of God are a broken spirit: a broken and a contrite heart, O God, thou wilt not despise." Unlike the man whose ambitions are dashed by overwhelming adversities, the man who is deeply wounded by God can claim the promise of Psalm 147:3, "He healeth the broken in heart, and bindeth up their wounds."

Brokenness is the way to blessing—the path away from the misguided self-reliance that ignores the tender mercies of God. The unbroken man, when sorely tried, can become a bitter man. The broken man has learned that the fiery trial does not make him what he ought to be, but rather it reveals what he is, so that God can make him what he wills the man to be. The broken man has learned to rejoice in the knowledge that the refining fire is temporary, though necessary to consume the dross, and to produce the faith that is much more precious than gold.

Better to Be Broken is the story of a man who has learned these truths—a man who learned the joy of a broken and contrite heart through the pain and hardship of a broken body. Through the author's transparency, the lessons of brokenness unfold with tears and laughter. Beneath a story of pain and suffering, of years of adaptation to new limitations, lies the unwavering faithfulness of a wife who tenderly loves a broken man, of daughters who joyfully ignore the wheelchair, and keep their eyes on "Dad,"—the unwritten illustration of our need to love and trust our Heavenly Father. In truth, *Better to Be Broken* is more than the story of a man; it is the story of a family whom God has wounded deeply, and is now using greatly.

Dr. John C. Vaughn
Author, *More Precious than Gold*

1

THERE HAS BEEN AN ACCIDENT

When the cargo door hit me, it compressed my spine and shattered three of my vertebrae. The small pieces of bone acted like razor blades, severing my spinal cord at the T8 level and leaving me with no movement or sensation below my eighth thoracic vertebra, or about the middle of my ribcage.

That happened on Wednesday afternoon. I awoke on Friday to a very different world, with no memory of the accident. The term paraplegia would now have a new meaning for me, but thanks to the "wonderful" effects of morphine and numerous other modern drugs, I didn't yet know nor even particularly care what that meant.

———

People are amazing. Some of them move through the motions of life with their eyes closed, never realizing how fragile they are. I was one of them. I had always been healthy. I stayed active, enjoyed hard work, and preferred doing everything myself. In essence, I thought I was ten feet tall and bulletproof. I did not need anyone or anything, and I gloried in that self-satisfaction.

On May 14, 1997, God allowed something to happen that made me see how blind I had been to the evil desires of my own heart. I was in the Air Force Reserve finishing up two weeks of active duty training at Dobbins Air Reserve Base in Marietta, Georgia. I was learning how to load cargo into the back of a C-130 trainer cargo plane. We were at the end of our last day of training before we would take the final test. My team decided to do one more load, and I volunteered to act as loadmaster. That meant I would stand in the back of the plane and guide the forklift driver who would move the pallets loaded with cargo.

The rear cargo door on a C-130 weighs approximately two tons and is raised up into the ceiling of the plane with a large central hydraulic piston. The planes are scheduled to have regular maintenance checks in order to make sure that all systems are functioning properly and that the large locking mechanism (called an up-lock) is working correctly. Once the door is raised in the up position, the up-lock is the only thing holding it in place. However, because these were C-130 trainers, proper maintenance checks had not been done on the hydraulic system or on the up-lock. I was standing under the cargo door directing the loading when a hydraulic line failure occurred, causing an up-lock failure. Suddenly and without warning, the two-ton door slammed down on the top of my head.

While all of this was happening in Georgia, my wife Wendy and my two daughters, Kara and Ariel, were at our home in South Berwick, Maine. They were getting ready for Wednesday evening prayer meeting at church. When the phone rang, little did Wendy realize how much her world was about to change. A representative of the Air Force told her solemnly, "There has been an accident and your husband is severely injured. You'll need to come to Georgia immediately."

Wendy tried to find out what had happened, but most of her questions went unanswered. The man did not know the details of the accident, only that it was extremely serious and that Wendy needed to come immediately. Our daughters, ages six and nine, stood by watching quietly. They could tell from their mother's end of the conversation that something was very wrong. After Wendy hung up the phone, she sat down with the girls. She explained that I had been hurt and that she had to fly to Georgia to be by my side. Our older daughter, Kara, began to cry. Ariel retreated to the kitchen without saying a word.

Wendy's mind was foggy as she struggled with what to do next. She knew my parents must be told, and so she picked up the receiver to make the dreaded call. My dad answered the phone, and Wendy did her best to explain what little she knew. The news hit my dad so hard that he was unable to tell my mom. She actually had to call Wendy back in order to find out what had happened. Wendy asked my mother if she would fly to Georgia with her. With anxious tears, my mom agreed.

Wendy then called her own parents who were already at the Wednesday night prayer meeting. They shared the heartbreaking news with their church family and then left to be with Wendy and the girls. Before long, phones were ringing all over the world with the news. It wasn't that I knew so many people but that I had one incredibly huge extended family—the family of God. Family, friends, and hundreds of church groups began praying for me that night.

The American Red Cross arranged a Thursday morning flight for Wendy and my mother. Numbly, Wendy made the necessary preparations and began packing for the trip. Then she found Ariel drawing at the kitchen table.

"What are you drawing, Ariel?" Wendy asked gently.

"Daddy," Ariel said as she picked up the sheet of paper and handed it to her mother. "Can you give it to him?"

It was a six-year-old's version of her daddy sitting in a wheelchair. No one knew at that moment how prophetic Ariel's picture would turn out to be.

The next day Wendy and Mom flew to Atlanta. It was very late when they landed, and they were both exhausted, but they were relieved when they were met by an Air Force sergeant who drove them to Kennestone Hospital. It was after 11:00 p.m. when the anxious pair made their way down the hospital corridor to the ICU. The nurses who met them were efficient but also friendly and empathetic to the situation. They explained that the visit could only be a couple of minutes, and then ushered my wife and mother into a sterile environment filled with all sorts of unfamiliar machines. They found me asleep in a strange-looking rotating bed and were overwhelmed by the seriousness of my condition. What could they say to me? "I'm sure you are going to be just fine," was unthinkable.

The nurses woke me up briefly, and I remember seeing Wendy on one side and Mom on the other. None of us remember any conversation other than two simple words that I said before I drifted out of consciousness—"I'm scared."

Following the short visit, the women left the hospital, and the sergeant drove them to a nearby hotel. Once inside their room, Mom collapsed into a chair and broke down. She was in an unfamiliar place surrounded by strangers. Coming from a small town in Maine to the large city of Atlanta, and seeing her oldest son barely alive and scared, was more than she could bear.

Wendy remained quiet with her own thoughts as they both tried to get some sleep. As she lay in bed that night, she remembered her recent prayers. She had asked God to bring something into my life that would turn my heart back to him and to our marriage. She remembered Romans 8:28, "And we know that all things work together for good to them that love God, to them who are the called according to his purpose." Could something as horrible as what she had witnessed in the hospital a few hours earlier be the answer to that prayer?

When they returned to the hospital the next morning and met with a doctor, the news was not good. He was not optimistic about my survival. If I did live, I would be in the hospital a very long time. I had head trauma and was paralyzed from the chest down. The doctor had no specific diagnosis but indicated that my broken back was probably the cause of my paralysis. He could not rule out brain damage.

Back in Maine, my dad had been a complete wreck as he waited and wondered about my fate. My parents' church family was incredible. Everyone jumped in to watch out for Dad. They brought meals, came to visit, and made phone calls. But while that helped greatly, everyone knew he needed to be in Georgia to see me and to support Mom.

At the same time, Wendy's dad was not only upset

about my accident but also burdened about his daughter's well-being. Day and night, he paced the floor and worried. After hearing the doctor's initial assessment, the two men agreed to fly to Georgia together. Facing the grim news head-on was better than staying at home worrying about the unknown. They made flight arrangements to join us the next week at Eisenhower Medical Center at Fort Gordon, Georgia, where I was to be transferred. My mother-in-law stayed in New Hampshire with our daughters, who were still in school nearby.

Slowly I began to wake up as my medications were gradually decreased. I found myself on the rotating bed, my wife standing on one side of me and my mother on the other. I had no sense of time. It seemed as if I had just seen them and told them, "I'm scared." As I began to understand where I was and to witness the fear in their eyes, I decided that my own fear was not an option. I determined that practical common sense and false bravado would get me through this. I had no idea how wrong I was.

As the days dragged on, I struggled with fear of what was ahead. As I lay in the ICU, my thoughts ran rampant. Am I dying? Will I ever get out of this bed? Is Wendy going to leave me? I tried to smile on the outside, but my mind was tormented with these questions—especially the one about losing Wendy.

Of course, after fifteen years I now realize that most of those thoughts were either drug induced or the result of the fear I was trying to deny. In time, I realized that I had been living my life with no personal responsibility or accountability to others. Slicing through the haze I was in, the cutting edge of truth came to me. I was not alone! God's presence became real like never before. I clung to the few Bible verses that I knew and prayed for strength for all of us. I knew that God was in control, and I rested in that fact. Nevertheless, accepting responsibility would be a new experience for me—one I would have to face head-on if I were ever to understand the true purpose of my life. I had been running away from responsibility for years. Now I would never run at all. Now I would have to learn the hard but necessary lessons.

2

WHO AM I?

So many things come into our lives to shape and mold us into our own unique person. Our early years are an important factor in this process—mine certainly were. As a child, I attended church with my family. My parents, various Sunday School teachers, and my pastor had taught me the Bible. At the age of ten, I realized what salvation was all about and that I needed it. I didn't understand all of the theology nor was it a great emotional experience for me, but I knew that I needed to have a personal relationship with Jesus Christ.

When my pastor showed me God's simple plan of salvation from the Bible, I saw that God loved me so much that he sent his only Son to take the punishment for my sin so that I would not have to take on the punishment myself. All I had to do was believe it and accept it. I followed Christ's own words: "For whosoever shall call upon the name of the Lord shall be saved" (Romans 10:13). While I am confident I became a Christian that day, I still had lots to learn before I grasped what living for God was all about.

———

I grew up on a type of farm. Grandparents, uncles, aunts, and cousins all lived on family property that had been divided. My grandfather had his own small lumber mill and cider press for the apple orchard. We also had huge gardens to take care of, shared beef cattle and hogs for butchering, and chickens for laying and eating. On top of that, my family burned about fourteen cords of wood a winter for heat. So, guess what we did all summer and fall? Hence, I was taught a strong work ethic from the time I was little.

From as early as I can remember, my parents made me feel good about almost everything I did. I seemed to be one of those people that got thrust into the lime-light a lot, and I learned to love praise and accolades from adults. I guess it made up for disappointments with my peers. In a small church like the one I grew up in, any amount of talent was appreciated. I started playing the piano when I was five. I always got the lead role in plays. I sang in the choir and even performed so-los. Because I had no understanding at that age where my gifts came from, the deadly sin of pride thrived in fertile soil. Someone else growing up in this same envi-ronment may not have let it go to their head like I did, and I certainly could not blame my family for how I reacted. It all made me think I was something special, and that attitude only served later to alienate me from my peers.

Coming from a middle-class Christian family, I am not an only child, and as the oldest, I always desired to be at the front of the line. My family and church en-couraged me always to do my best to serve others. Yet, I never personally tempered my best with any sense of humility.

My mom and dad were my biggest cheerleaders. I never once doubted their love. Everything they did was focused on what they felt was best for me and my two younger brothers. We were taught that anything worth doing is worth doing right the first time. We were al-ways active in church, and serving others was a way of life for all of us.

Our hometown was an average small New England

community originally settled by a handful of families in the 1600s or thereabouts. Most settlers arrived in the colonies as indentured servants, subsistence farmers, or tradesmen. They built settlements and remained there for generations, but there was nothing to have earned the majority of them any bragging rights. The Huntress family of Shapleigh, Maine, happened to be among those that traced their roots to those early beginnings.

Growing up in a town of only nine hundred people was like the childhood game "king of the hill." Descendants of the oldest families were active in town politics, local businesses, community functions, and the church. There always seemed to be an undercurrent by which one family tried to "best" the others. I was very much a part of this game and I played it well—even among my school buddies. One year the Huntress family might secure their place on top of the heap—the next year another Shapleigh clan would knock us off!

Growing up with this king-of-the-hill mentality gave me a false sense of self-importance. By the world's standards, I am a type A personality and a "natural leader." So, in comfortable surroundings—elementary school, home, church—I was looked upon as the leader, and I fit readily into that role.

The day came, however, when I was forced to compete for leadership positions. I remember very well the first time the reality of my own insignificance hit me. I was entering my first year of junior high school. I had been thrown into a consolidated district school comprised of students from seven surrounding towns. Suddenly, I felt like a very small fish in a much bigger pond than Shapleigh Elementary School. A group of seventh graders helped me understand right from the start that my family and our name were no big deal! I suddenly found myself being led instead of leading. Rather than being humbled and using my gifts and talents for the glory of God, I began to push harder at the things I was good at in order to be better than the next one in line.

I was not good looking, athletic, or scholastically gifted, and I actually enjoyed going to church. I had none of the qualities that made the average junior high student popular or well liked, but popularity was very important to me. So, for the next six years I became an actor, a fake, a superb liar, an expert at hiding the real Rick Huntress.

This way of thinking soon controlled my entire life. My focus was no longer on pleasing God but rather on doing whatever it took to get what I wanted and to go where I wanted to go. Once, when a kid on our school bus laughed at the way I pronounced a particular word, the incident drove me to begin reading the dictionary so that I could speak correctly. If there was anything I needed to do to improve what others thought of me, I was determined to do it.

As time went on, the person that I thought I was—the person that I wanted to be—was swallowed up in his own weaknesses. I became bitter, angry, scared, and worst of all, someone that I no longer recognized. With every difficult circumstance that came my way, I built a new wall to hide behind. Revealing my hurt meant that I was weak, and that did not make me look like a man. I was building a fortress constructed of arrogance and pride. It served me well—protecting me from revealing how much I hurt inside. The desire to conceal the real me kept me from standing up for my belief in God and the decision I had made when I was ten years old. When faced with difficulties and temptations, I acted like anything but a Christian.

I paid close attention to people I thought had "made it" in the world—how they acted, dressed, carried themselves. As I focused on acting like those who were high up in the world's eyes, I slipped further and further away from the values I had learned at home and at church. I was blinded to the truth that it was God who had given me my abilities—that my talents were a gift from him and were to be used to glorify him. As a result, I took something good and corrupted it almost to a point of no return.

I wanted acceptance and friends more than all else and was determined to have them. I sacrificed anything in order to get them. Consumed with selfishness, I resolved to "show them all." After graduating from high school, I'd leave Shapleigh, leave Maine, leave all of New England for that matter. I would run away from everything and everyone that had caused my hurt. But, I was taking the cause with me, and run as I might, I could never outrun myself!

In September of 1979, I headed off to the University of Maine, housed on a beautiful campus in Orono, on the banks of the Stillwater River. While I wouldn't be getting out of New England after all, that was okay. I could hardly wait for this new start and what I thought were unlimited opportunities to have fun. At first everything was great. There were plenty of occasions to hike the network of recreational trails, to mountain climb, and to hang out with friends—all things I loved. I reveled in my newfound manhood and put my junior high and high school years behind me.

But soon the same self-centered "actor" I thought I had left in Shapleigh showed up again on the center stage of my life. I saw what was happening, but I never once considered what I was doing to my soul. When I had trouble, I blamed others. I did not feel an ounce of personal responsibility or accountability for my actions. My solutions for handling problems at college drew me deeper into trouble because I had no family support to keep me in check.

Majoring in biology, I enjoyed the science, anatomy, and psychology classes. We were taught that who we are is determined by our environment, the way we are brought up, or by genetics. I found the classes interesting and started out strong academically. But I fizzled out quickly because academics were at the bottom of my priority list. I rarely thought about important matters. I was in the business of achieving popularity regardless of what it took or what types of people I had to associate with in order to gain it.

The fraternity groups, which my roommates were a part of, became my new friends. Instead of saying no to things that a Christian should avoid, I followed the crowd and forced myself to fit in where I did not. Many of the guys smoked, almost everyone drank, and if I didn't partake, they laughed at me. I had no desire to smoke or drink, but I was caught between what I wanted and what I had to do to get it. I chose the middle of the road. I made excuses, lied, and avoided the very "friends" I wanted to impress. Before long, I became a recluse with no friends. Many considered me a snob (high school all over again!). I preferred to have them think of me as a snob than as a Christian. It never occurred to me to find a good church and make friends with other believers who would help me grow.

During the summer between my freshman and sophomore years in college, I met Wendy. I had been home for the summer and was attending church with my parents. We had a small congregation, so it was impossible to miss visitors, especially if they showed up late and were forced to sit in the front row. I sang in the choir that summer. As we always did, we walked into the sanctuary at the beginning of the service and faced the congregation. There she was, this beautiful young lady wearing a maroon dress sitting in the first pew only two feet in front of me!

I remember it like it was yesterday. She had long blonde hair, blue eyes, a terrific figure, and a winning smile. She was, no doubt, one of the many summer visitors that came to our church each year, but I had never noticed her before. She stood out from the usual girls I knew at school who wore mostly blue jeans and sweatshirts and had no desire to look or act feminine. I determined to meet this girl, and I spent the entire service planning my strategy.

When the pastor said the final amen, everyone started filing out the front door while I quickly ditched my choir robe and headed out the back door. I was hoping to catch her in the parking lot before she left. As she was getting into her grandmother's car, I ran up to her, said a quick "hi," welcomed her to church, and even invited her to our Sunday afternoon softball game. She said "hi" back and "thank you" and got in the car. As the family drove off, I thought what a complete fool I had made of myself. Later in the day, when she didn't show for the softball game, I was sure of it. I assumed I would never see her again.

But that was not to be. The two of us bumped into each other a few more times over the summer, and I finally worked up enough courage to ask her out on a date. I was amazed when she actually showed interest in me and said yes. I invited her to an upscale restaurant in an attempt to impress her but also figured it would give us some time to talk. I found out that she was only sixteen and attended a private Christian boarding school for high school students in Dublin, New Hampshire, about two hours from Rochester where her family lived. They had a summer home in Shapleigh on one of the many lakes in our area and were there on summer vacation. Wendy looked to be about nineteen—my age—so I felt a little nervous when I realized that she was three years younger.

As we continued talking, I sensed in her qualities that were truly attractive. Not only was she beautiful, she was down to earth, the perfect lady, and very easy to laugh with. From the beginning, it was clear that Wendy had a strong faith in Christ. However, while we had Christ in common, I knew that my faith was somewhere on a back shelf. Yet, something told me that Wendy was evidence of God's grace to me and proof that he was not through with me yet.

During the fall semester when I began my sophomore year at the university, she left for boarding school six hours away, so we were not able to see much of each other. There were no cell phones then, and I had no money for long distance calls. Letter writing was our only option, and I believe it was that single factor that protected me from destroying our relationship. My self-serving nature had not changed, but I was able to portray in writing the man I wished I was. I knew there was something very special about Wendy. I also realized she was not getting to know the real Rick Huntress but rather the guy I wanted her to know. While I knew this was not the way to build a healthy relationship and that it was unfair to Wendy, somehow we continued dating. Soon we had fallen in love, but it was the untested love of a sixteen- and nineteen-year-old.

I lasted a year and a half at the University of Maine. Then, applying the same reasoning I used when I left home, I decided to spread my wings—to fly wherever my selfish desires took me. That brilliant, and as I look back now, ironic decision led me to enlist in the Air Force. Because I went in on the delayed enlistment program, I moved back to Shapleigh with my parents for a couple of months before heading off to basic training. Wendy and I had been dating for about eight months when the time came for me to leave for the Air Force. Our relationship continued, but since we now saw even less of each other, our letter writing became more frequent.

The three years that Wendy and I dated gave us time to see the good and not so good in each other. In my heart, I knew that Wendy was the type of girl I wanted as a wife. Not only was she beautiful, she was also gracious and charming. She knew which fork to use at a fancy dinner and actually enjoyed being feminine. However, I saw these traits in a selfish way. Wendy would help me to get ahead professionally. People noticed this charming lady, and I knew she would be a great asset to me in opening doors of opportunity wherever my career took me.

It is important to understand what I am saying here. I loved Wendy very much and still do. There is no room for doubt about that aspect of our relationship. I have always been amazed that she loved me back. However, in order to share the full message of what God has done in my life, I feel it necessary to confess that I also saw in Wendy a woman who could help me move ahead in life, both socially and materially.

Wendy and I were married on September 3, 1983. Following the wedding, we left Maine for Illinois, where I was stationed at Chanute Air Force Base. I was twenty-two, married to the most gorgeous, charming, loving woman in the world, and twelve hundred miles from my past. We were living life to the fullest. Everything was perfect, at last. At that time, Shakespeare's well-written words were the furthest thing from my mind: "Lord, what fools these mortals be."

At that point in my life I had everything a man could want in this world. Yet I was still not content. The strong cords of selfishness, arrogance, and pride had me bound, and they shaped every decision that I made. They had followed me from New England, through my short college stint, and were now evident in my new life with Wendy. While she should have been my number one priority, my wife soon took a back seat to my personal ambitions. I resumed my old habits—seeking friends among the perceived "achievers"—regardless of what types of people they happened to be.

While on active duty, I became a technical instructor for the school of electronics at Chanute Air Force Base. This was a step up from my original assignment as an avionics technician. Along with my new job came nice perks like base housing, working in an office, and regular Monday thru Friday hours. I held that job the entire time I was on active duty, and it fueled my desire to work in the white-collar world.

After serving out my active duty commitment, I remained in the Air Force Reserve, and Wendy and I moved back to Maine. Through her family connections, I got a job at a local bank. I enjoyed the work but soon realized that to continue my climb up the corporate ladder, I would need a college degree. Wendy and her family suggested that I attend Bob Jones University in Greenville, South Carolina. I had never heard of it before I met Wendy, but the prestige of attending a private university appealed to me. I considered going there because it fit my desire for status. The fact that it was a Christian college played only a minor role in that consideration.

While we were in Maine, Wendy had three miscarriages and was told that she would not be able to carry a baby full term. We were heartbroken and decided it was time for me to go back to school to finish my degree. So, in 1986, we packed up and moved to Greenville. I attended school full time, choosing to major in business this time around. I found a part-time job working for a large bank at their Greenville operations center. I loved my new job and felt like I was moving up in the world.

Less than a year later, God gave us an answer to prayer when our oldest daughter Kara was born. Since Wendy and I both desired she be a stay-at-home mom with our new baby, I once again quit college to work full time. The bank I worked for offered me a huge promotion to their corporate headquarters in Charlotte, North Carolina, and I jumped at the chance.

While living in Charlotte we were blessed with a second daughter, Ariel. We lived in Charlotte for eight years, and during that time I pushed and maneuvered my way up the corporate ladder. I willingly compromised my Christian values in order to achieve what I had convinced myself was the all-important goal in life—my personal ambition.

Although Wendy's gentle and loving spirit was slowly having an impact on me, I continued to pursue what I wanted. There were so many things I hated about the man I had become. I wanted to change but failed repeatedly. There is a well-known phrase among Christians: "I fell into sin." But, may I say, "Rick Huntress never once fell into sin—he had both eyes wide open and jumped right in with both feet." As a Christian, I knew that I needed to change. I also knew that

I could not change on my own—I needed God's help. But I had no idea how to get it.

Over the years, God sent many things into my life to remind me that I should live for him, for my family, and for others. But I chose to ignore God. I fixed my eyes on the corporate ladder and chased after worldly desires and ambitions. I flew around the country on corporate jets, partook in social drinking, and attended fancy parties. Wendy wanted no part of this life, and the tension in our marriage grew. I began to see my wife as a liability rather than as an asset. Where I had expected her to help me move ahead, she was holding me back. In 1995, with no thought of anyone but myself, I told Wendy that I wanted a separation. While she was not surprised, Wendy was still devastated over where I had taken our marriage. She asked me if I wanted a divorce. Strangely enough, I did not. My life was a mess at that point. I was clueless about what I wanted. So Wendy and our daughters moved back to New Hampshire with her parents, and I stayed in Charlotte.

Over the next year and a half Wendy and I talked, received marriage counseling, and continued to see each other. Our love was still alive, and we decided to fight for our marriage and family. My love for Wendy and our daughters drove me to resign from my job in North Carolina. We sold our house, and I moved back to South Berwick, Maine. But while I brought with me a deep desire to salvage our family, I had not let go of the man I had become. It was still all about me. Wendy and I both knew that if something did not change at the very deepest level of my being, we were in serious trouble of losing everything.

———

Yes, many things in our life shape and mold the person we eventually become. I wondered, "Who am I? What am I?" I hadn't bothered to think that deeply back when I was a kid in Shapleigh. Like most people, I had heard the tried and true (and sometimes not so true) sayings like, "Oh, you can't help it. You are just like your father," or "Red hair—red hot temper!" But while I heard them, I never gave much thought to how they affected me personally. Even the college psychology course I took at the university had not provoked me to ponder my belief system to any great degree.

Was there no responsibility for the character of the guy that looked back at me in the mirror every morning? If I held to the belief of behaviorism, then I was simply a trained monkey that performed in a certain way due to many years of training and influence from family, friends, and educators. If I held to the belief of determinism, I had no choice but to follow my carnal instincts and do anything necessary to satisfy myself. But if I was a Christian, how did my belief system fit into the very confusing jigsaw puzzle that was me?

On May 14, 1997, God began to break me. My life was about to take a drastic turn for the better.

3

A RIDE TO FORGET

When I finally woke up in that hospital in Atlanta, Georgia, I learned that there was hope. The medical staff scheduled me for surgery the following week. I wondered why they put it off until then. Perhaps the doctors wanted to make sure that I would appreciate their investment of time—that I wouldn't be an ingrate and die on them!

My accident happened on Wednesday at Dobbins Air Reserve Base, which is right outside of Atlanta, Georgia, so I had been rushed to a local hospital. I remained there until Saturday, May 17, when the Air Force moved me to Eisenhower Medical Center at Fort Gordon in Augusta, Georgia, 160 miles away.

Someone in the military chain of command made the decision to use a medical transport service to move me rather than to use Medivac to fly me in by helicopter. Wendy and Mom thought that was a bad idea. So did some of the attending nurses. All questions concerning me were directed to Wendy. She was at a loss on how to deal with the military. When she was told that ground transport was being lined up to move me, she agreed without question. She remembers looking to me for direction several times, which of course did not help. I was in severe pain, in and out of consciousness, and was for the most part out of touch with what was going on around me. As a result of our hesitation, a few problems were not taken into consideration by the doctors when the decision was made. For example, a transport service is not allowed to administer medication. Because of that, my morphine pump was removed. That meant I would not receive any pain medication until I reached the hospital at Fort Gordon, which was nearly three hours away. As it turned out, that was the least of my problems.

The enormity of the mistake to use that transport service became apparent to me as I was moved from the hospital bed to the gurney, then bounced into the transport vehicle. My pain became more and more excruciating with each passing minute and with each tormenting bounce. Since it was a Saturday, the driver was more interested in enjoying her weekend than in driving a half-dead body across Georgia. And the pièce de résistance was that the transport service had only one vehicle available, and it had its own disability—the air conditioning did not work! As anyone who is from the South knows, the end of May in Georgia can be stifling, and that particular day was no exception.

The medical workers took me out of an air-conditioned ICU, packed me into the back of an "oven on wheels" with Wendy and a male attendant, and down the road we went. It didn't take long to recognize the horrific inefficiency of the transport service. Incredibly, we had to make a fuel stop on the way. Dodging in and out of traffic and rapidly switching lanes, the driver flew into the first service station she came to.

"We are going to have to go to another station!" the driver yelled to the attendant in the back. "This one doesn't have diesel!"

So the driver jerked the ambulance back into the heavy Atlanta traffic to look for a second service station with diesel fuel. When she found one, she bounced the vehicle over the sidewalk to get to the fuel pump! My entire body throbbed with pain as I was bounced unmercifully in the back of the transport.

Because my pain had reached unbearable levels at this point of the trip, the remainder of the trip to Fort Gordon is a little fuzzy in my memory. I am relying on others to relate the rest of this "adventure." In order to make up for lost time at the gas pumps, the driver appeared to see how fast she could cover 160 miles of interstate between Atlanta and Augusta. There we were, speeding down the interstate, while the transport driver was applying polish to her fingernails—apparently oblivious to the cargo at the back of the transport!

While the male attendant and my wife tried their best to prevent me from bouncing, an Air Force sergeant and my mother attempted to follow us in a separate car. They were speechless over what they were seeing. The sergeant did his best to stay with the transport. However, once the driver made it onto the interstate, the sergeant watched our vehicle disappear into the distance like he was sitting still. Mom remembers glancing at the speedometer, and when she saw the needle pointing to 105 mph, she gasped in horror!

"How fast are we going?" she asked in sheer terror.

"One hundred five miles per hour, but the ambulance is leaving us in its dust," the sergeant replied.

Through clenched teeth she told the sergeant he should be very thankful that he was not her husband, because if he was, she would kill him. Knowing that my mother gets nervous doing 55 mph, I don't think her statement was too far removed from the truth.

Meanwhile, back in the transport vehicle, the heat and motion got the better of me, and I began to throw up. I panicked from the pain and lack of air in the back. That added to the frustration and concern of the attendant and Wendy who were making every effort to hold me in place.

The driver's lack of concern for the situation distracted her from seeing a large log in our lane of traffic. We hit the log at rocket speed, and the impact caused the underside of the transport to burst into flames!

Wendy just closed her eyes. All she could think about at that moment was that we were all going to die. But once again, God had other plans, and we eventually skidded to a stop on the edge of the pavement.

"This is not MY fault!" the driver yelled.

When she tried to radio for assistance, she found that her radio was not working. So the attendant and my wife pulled me out of the back of the transport and quickly rolled me down the freeway on my gurney away from the smoking vehicle, as I continued to have dry heaves in between periods of unconsciousness from the tormenting pain. While the driver and attendant were in a heated argument over what to do next, the highway became clogged with traffic stopped to see what had happened.

When the Air Force sergeant, along with my extremely distraught mother, showed up on the scene, they had no way of calling for assistance either. Thankfully, someone from the crowd of people that had gathered to stare at the show produced a cell phone and was able to call for an ambulance. Once it arrived, I was put into the most wonderful air conditioning I had ever felt. And since this was a real ambulance, the medical assistants were allowed to administer medication. They gave me a shot that completely knocked me out for the rest of the trip. When I awoke I was in a new ICU, back on my morphine pump, and in my rotating bed. Life was good.

4
THE MAKING OF A MAN

The ICU at Eisenhower Medical Center was similar to the hospital that I had just left. I was placed in a Stryker rotating bed, and when I opened my eyes I saw Wendy on one side and Mom on the other. As before, I was attached to a morphine pump, IVs, monitors, and tubes of all sorts and sizes. Soft beeps and buzzers came from the state-of-the-art medical equipment around me.

My wife and family were allowed only short visits, so the rest of the time I lay in the bed rotating from side to side and listening. I heard nurses and doctors talking. I heard moaning, screaming, and crying. I heard constant movement around me as nurses added a new IV bag, gave me a shot, or performed many other tasks that I did not understand. Listening to the screams of people in nearby beds was awful. Yet, in that sterile environment there was an alarming silence at the same time. The silence was often worse than the cries of anguish, for that often meant that yet another patient had not made it. I wondered if I might be next.

For the most part, I remained quiet, speaking only when spoken to, not because I was bitter or angry, but because I didn't want to think about my new reality. Heavily sedated, I allowed myself to retreat into hazy oblivion.

As the week dragged on, the doctors began to prepare me for surgery. They explained the basics of the operation and what they hoped to accomplish, but they left the details very sketchy. I assumed they were telling Wendy more than they were telling me, so I wasn't too worried about it. Later, I found out that they had told

Wendy even less than they had told me. The one thing I do remember was that they told me that I had a fifty-fifty chance of surviving the surgery.

My fear increased because I was not allowed to talk with my two daughters, Kara and Ariel, before the operation. There were so many things I wanted to tell my girls—how much I loved them, how much I knew I had let them down. I feared I would never have an opportunity to tell them I was sorry and to ask for their forgiveness.

Wendy and I discussed very little of consequence while we waited. When Dad and my father-in-law arrived, I was encouraged. I knew it was good for Wendy and Mom to have them by their side, but I could tell from looking at my dad that seeing his son like this was killing him. Yet, he was his usual giving self, and he became a source of stability and strength for all of us. Wendy tried to remain calm, and I attempted to keep up a good front for my wife and parents. But I saw the fear in everyone's eyes and heard it in their forced banter.

Filling out advance directives for my wishes in case of complications during the surgery, I chose to die if something went wrong. I forced a smile and signed my name.

Wendy understood my decision and why I made it. We discussed it even though she did not want to think about the reality of it, but she respected my choice. My parents were a different story. The doctors had told them the seriousness of the surgery and the many things that could go wrong, and Mom could not bring herself to accept what I was signing. She felt like she was watching her child die and could do nothing about it. Mom wanted assurance from the doctors that they would do what was necessary to keep me alive. The best she could get was that they would do their best for me to make it off the operating table. With a fearful heart and tears in her eyes, all she could say was, "Thank you."

On the day of my surgery, I asked if I could call my daughters who were still in New Hampshire with Wendy's mom. I was not allowed to make the call, so Wendy promised to call the girls as soon as possible to tell them I loved them. The doctor expected the surgery to last about six hours and assured me he would contact the family as soon as the operation was over. I got a kiss from Wendy and one from my mother, and then was taken away to an unknown future. I watched the ceiling lights going by as the orderlies rolled me down the hall. Closing my eyes, I prayed for strength and peace to fill my heart to replace the fear that threatened to crush me. The mild sedative put in my IV before I was taken to the operating room began to work. I said goodbye to Wendy. That is the last thing I remember.

After six hours of surgery there was no word. My mother had refused to leave the waiting room until they received news of the outcome. So Wendy and her dad, my parents, and two Air Force sergeants—who had been assigned to never leave my family's side—waited for news and feared the worst. In Maine my brothers, Bruce and Steve, sat by their phones anxiously waiting.

Bruce and his wife Nancy had one son. Steve and his wife Denise had a girl and a boy. All of them were in shock over my accident. Since my brothers and I had our own families, jobs, and friends, we didn't see a lot of each other but were busy racing through life. Now that race seemed unimportant to all of us. Bruce and Steve were the points of contact for our grandparents, our aunts and uncles, our cousins, and many churches and friends. They did their best to keep everyone up to date on what was happening in Georgia. Wendy's sister Vicki, along with her husband Paul and one daughter, were missionaries who traveled the United States, as Paul served as a chalk artist in evangelism. With so many points of contact from Wendy's family and mine, literally thousands of people prayed for me throughout the day—and waited.

As the seemingly endless waiting dragged on, fear and doubt gripped my loved ones. They went without food and drank hospital coffee, watching for the surgeon to come down the hall. There were so many things that could go wrong. The more time that passed, the more they imagined the worst.

Finally, after thirteen long hours, the surgeon appeared, spoke briefly to the family, and told Wendy that it was important that she go in and see me right away. "Your presence at this point is crucial if your husband is to survive," he said.

As the doctor ushered Wendy to the recovery area, he once again explained the seriousness of my injury and how traumatizing the surgery had been on my body. "It is extremely important that you remain calm and reassuring," he instructed her.

Sensing that I was at death's door and anxious to see me, Wendy followed the doctor to my bedside. Had the doctor not told her it was so, she would not have known it was me lying there. I was on a breathing tube, deathly white, my entire body swollen—with no recognizable facial features. The doctor told Wendy that they had paralyzed my arms temporarily in order to keep me still.

Wendy stared in disbelief, struggling in uncertainty to find the words to say to me. As she approached the bed, she began to talk softly. At that moment, my arms flew up and grabbed her head in a frightening, vise-like grip. Hadn't she just been told that I was unable to move? She continued talking to me as the doctor peeled my arms away. After only a few minutes, the nurse asked her to leave. Still in shock, Wendy returned to the waiting room to talk with the family—and fainted.

Although I remembered none of this, the family would tell me later. My first memories of that day are that I could not see or move my arms. Because of the breathing tube, I was unable to speak. Fear and panic held me in a swirl of total confusion. Worse, I could not ask the questions that caused my panic: Why can't I see? Why can't I move my arms? Has something gone wrong? Am I on life support? Why didn't they just let me die?

Paralyzed and alone, the only thing I could do was to let the tears roll down my face. Hour after hour, I prayed and cried to God to let me die. But God wouldn't take my life, and I couldn't.

Over the next several hours, the medical personnel began to cut back on my sedation. I heard the doctor talking to me and explaining how the surgery went.

He hoped to remove the breathing tube as soon as I was stable. Gradually, I could move my arms, but they were strapped to my sides because I fought to pull out the breathing tube. I had never had surgery and had no idea what to expect. I didn't know that a breathing tube was standard protocol; I resented that the doctors had not better prepared me for all of this.

After what seemed like an eternity but was actually the next day, the doctor removed my breathing tube. It felt like rolled-up sandpaper being dragged out of my throat. I still could not speak but managed to whisper in a raspy voice, "I want to see Wendy."

She was my anchor in a turbulent sea of despair. I was lost without her. Wendy had been allowed to see me only briefly in recovery when I was back in the ICU. A nurse had stayed with me throughout the night, never leaving my bedside. As my body tried to shut down, the nurse kept waking me up to keep me breathing.

The Sunday following my surgery, I was allowed to see Wendy and my family, but no more than two at a time and only for thirty-minute sessions with long breaks between visits. I tried to keep a smile on my face and laugh politely at jokes. But my breathing was still shallow; fluid collected in my lungs. The doctors tried various medications on me, and the nurses encouraged me to cough and take deep breaths. I breathed; I coughed; I waited. This continued for a few days, but I slept very little. When I did pass out, it was due to the morphine, and I had a dreadful, recurring nightmare. In my nightmare I was lying in a large valley crowded with people paralyzed like me. The valley was lush and green, but we were all on drugs. The people seemed friendly and glad to have me with them as long as I made no attempt to leave the beautiful valley. But I desperately wanted to leave! I struggled against the drugs and tried to climb out, but the valley became a terrible pit, and the once-friendly people became hideous, screaming enemies that refused to let me go. They dragged me and pulled me back into the pit. Emotionally and spiritually, I was at the breaking point. When I was awake, I refused to mention the dream. My body was broken, but my willful heart kept up the act—I faked the smiles.

Finally, after days of pretense—forced smiles and horrible nightmares over and over—I knew I had reached the end of myself. One evening, when visiting hours were over, Wendy and my mother had just left the hospital for the night. My breathing had been exceptionally bad that day, and I was given a new medication through a breathing mask. I hoped it would help, but as I got more of the medication in my system, I panicked. Without warning, the emotional wall that I had built up around myself came crashing down. I ripped the mask off and started screaming. "I want Wendy! I NEED Wendy! I have to have Wendy!"

I could have stopped screaming if I had wanted to, but I didn't want to. The nurse explained that visiting hours were over and that it was not possible for Wendy to come back. With the doctor's permission, the nurse increased my morphine, but I continued to rant and rave until she finally gave in and agreed to send for Wendy if I would calm down. I settled down a bit, and in a few minutes the nurse returned to tell me that Wendy was on her way. However, I continued to thrash my arms and head, crying and babbling continuously.

When I heard Wendy's calming voice beside me, and I saw that my dad was with her, the dam burst. Every emotion that I had held in for the past two weeks gushed out of me. I was scared to death, in constant pain, I didn't understand things, and on and on and on I went. The last thing I screamed out to Wendy was that I was no longer a man! Then I broke down into uncontrollable sobbing. Wendy patiently tried to calm me down, and I slowly began to listen and stopped my outbursts.

Whenever two family members were in my room, one would be on one side of me and one would be on the other. Each time my bed rotated toward Wendy, she attempted to whisper something in my ear. But not until I had quieted down enough to listen to her did I realize what she was saying. Finally, I got it. In their haste to get to the hospital, my dad had hastily thrown his clothes on over his pajamas. He arrived at the hospital with his white hair standing straight up and his pajamas sticking out all over the place, unkempt and unzipped. Wendy was trying to tell me, in hopes that I would tell him. On the next rotation—my turn to face Dad—I nonchalantly told him to zip up. The tension was broken, and the three of us enjoyed a much-needed chuckle.

In spite of his wardrobe malfunction, Dad had the foresight to bring his Bible with him, and I asked him if he would please read me the Christmas story from

Luke. I wanted to hear something warm and comforting that would cover the horrible nightmare I was now living in. After reading the story, Dad called the Army chaplain, who immediately came to see how he could help. I had begun to cry and thrash around again when the chaplain arrived and asked, "What do you need in order to make it through this night—not tomorrow or the day after that, but this one night?"

I told him that I wanted Wendy to stay the night with me.

The chaplain left and made one quick phone call. When he returned, he said that my request was granted. After a while, Dad and the chaplain left, and Wendy sat in a straight-backed chair brought in for her. I continued to vent, and for the most part, I'm sure I made no sense at all. At a loss as to what she could do, Wendy began to sing old familiar hymns to me. The calming effect of her soothing voice was instant. I began to quiet down, stopped thrashing around, and with the help of the morphine, even drifted off. I would wake up in a panic, then hear Wendy singing softly, and calmness would wash over me. She sang to me throughout the night—from midnight to 6:00 a.m., holding my hand and gently stroking my face. When morning finally came, I was able to talk rationally with Wendy. Her faith and confidence in God gave her an incredible inner strength to endure what would have crushed most people. Her strength gave me strength.

Wendy's gentle way, her heartfelt prayers, and her unfailing love were holding me back from self-destruction. Everyone around us was amazed by her. I can never express to her, or to anyone else, how much she did for me that long, dreadful night. Years later I write with tears, remembering her sacrifice for me. That she loved me enough to do that even after everything I had put her through is more than I can comprehend. Wendy's sacrificial love for me was, and is, truly amazing. She gave of herself on that night in a way that clearly demonstrated the love that God has for each of us. The Bible tells us in Romans 3:10–12, "There is none righteous, no, not one: there is none that understandeth, there is none that seeketh after God. They are all gone out of the way, they are together become unprofitable; there is none that doeth good, no, not one." Yet God still loved all of us enough, even though we betrayed and disappointed him, to sacrifice his only Son. "While we were yet sinners, Christ died for us" (Romans 5:8).

At some point, the hospital psychiatrist told us that, statistically, seventy percent of all marriages in which a partner experiences a traumatic injury will end in divorce. Wendy could have chosen to leave me, just as God could have left us in our sin. But my wife chose to stay, following God's example of choosing a sacrifice beyond human understanding—his only Son. God's Word poses the question, "How shall we escape if we neglect so great salvation?" (Hebrews 2:3). God has given freely his gift of eternal life. All we have to do is accept it.

5
PERSONAL REFLECTION

In reality, that night was a turning point—the night when brokenness became evident. That crisis was good and necessary for me to go through. When Wendy left around 6:00 a.m. to go back to the hotel, she was emotionally and physically exhausted. But instead of crawling into bed for much-needed rest, she showered, ate breakfast, and returned with my parents to the hospital.

Explaining the change in me after that night requires transparency on my part. Because my body and mind were at a common breaking point brought on by medications and exhaustion, it would be natural to blame my outburst on my tragic circumstances. But this time it was my personal choice to let my feelings explode and take over instead of internalizing my feelings and remaining the stoic. Expressing how I felt to anyone, even Wendy, indicated in my mind that I was weak and not in control. My outburst had been embarrassing and extremely childlike. Although I paid lip service to God's control of my life before the crisis, I had not surrendered my stubborn will to Him. I hated the thought that others around me might see that I was not perfect, that my marriage was not perfect, and that my relationship with God was far from perfect.

In contrast, my emotional and physical weakness emphasized the strength that Wendy possessed. More importantly, I realized that her strength was rooted in her close and abiding relationship with God. A dear friend of mine and former high school teacher, who knows Wendy's family, once told me, "She comes from good stock." Truer words have never been spoken. Wendy has a love and inner strength that is a special gift from God. It cannot be mimicked by human effort.

When my accident happened, our marriage was already shaky. Had Wendy walked away from the nightmare, few people would have blamed her. Of course I loved Wendy, but I had never given her all of me. I was so afraid of getting hurt that I wasn't concerned about being completely honest with anyone. God alone could tear down the wall I had spent thirty-six years building. And that is exactly what he did.

Hebrews 12:5–7 tells us, "And ye have forgotten the exhortation which speaketh unto you as unto children, My son, despise not thou the chastening of the Lord, nor faint when thou art rebuked of him: For whom the Lord loveth he chasteneth, and scourgeth every son whom he receiveth. If ye endure chastening, God dealeth with you as with sons; for what son is he whom the father chasteneth not?" I wouldn't say that God caused my accident to happen, but he did allow it to happen. During the weeks after my surgery, as my body was physically healing, God knew that what I needed most was spiritual healing. That could only be accomplished by his direct hand. He brought me to a place in which rescue was possible only by complete trust in him. It had been so long since I had trusted him that I had forgotten how. But from the moment of the accident, the journey had begun.

On the day of the crisis, I began to understand that trusting is a journey—not one to dread but one to look forward to. When I finally surrendered, giving every part of my being to God, trusting that he would not hurt me, all of my other relationships came into focus. Wendy and I became closer than we had ever been, my family became more important than my career, and I began to discover innumerable things more important in life than trying to please the world. Transparency is never easy when we live in fear of getting hurt, but living life without trust and without God in control is impossible. That road leads to destruction. If we do not get off that road, it will bring eternal consequences.

What happened to me in the crisis was, in a way, much like salvation. In a sense I did enter into a "saving" relationship with Christ the night that I experienced what some would call an emotional breakdown. However, I remember very well accepting Jesus Christ as my Savior when I was ten years old—I had already been washed by his cleansing blood. Although the poor choices that I had made over the years had damaged my relationship with God, it could not be destroyed. There are many examples of damaged relationships with God in the Bible. One of the best known is the story of David with Bathsheba. David was devoted to serving God. In Acts 13:22, God calls David "a man after mine own heart." Yet, in spite of a personal and loving relationship with his heavenly father, David turned his eyes away from God, committing adultery, lying, and even murdering. But when David was confronted with his sins, he accepted responsibility for his actions and the consequences. When David wrote Psalm 51 he was a broken man with true repentance. In verses 10–12 he says, "Create in me a clean heart, O God; and renew a right spirit within me. Cast me not away from thy presence; and take not thy holy spirit from me. Restore unto me the joy of thy salvation; and uphold me with thy free spirit." How I love that word "renew"! Verse 17 of this same Psalm says, "The sacrifices of God are a broken spirit: a broken and a contrite heart, O God, thou wilt not despise." I, too, was broken, and it was the best thing that ever happened to me. My broken back is a blessing from God. He used it to bring me back to himself. I have heard it said, "God sometimes puts us flat on our back, so we can learn to look up at him." That certainly was true for me.

6

REHABILITATION

After eighteen days in the ICU at Eisenhower Medical Center, I was finally ready for my next challenge—rehabilitation. From the choice of locations available to do rehab, I chose the Veteran's Administration Hospital in West Roxbury, Massachusetts. It was closest to Maine, and I would be able to see my daughters. It had been three long weeks since the accident, and I was so excited to see them I could hardly wait to get on the plane!

My parents and father-in-law flew home on a commercial flight, while Wendy and I were taken on a Medivac flight. When we landed at Hanscom Air Field in Massachusetts, we were greeted on the tarmac by my entire family. I was deathly sick from the trip and in extreme pain, but I didn't care because of the hugs and kisses from my daughters. I got to see both of my brothers and their families as well. During the reunions, I could say nothing; all I could do was cry. After receiving more medication to knock me out, I was transported by ambulance to what I was told would be my new home for three to six months, depending on my progress in therapy.

The first few days were rough. After the long flight from Georgia, the emotional reunion, and the pain in my body, I was not ready for what rehabilitation involved. In severe pain, I was hooked up to all of the machines, IVs, and the morphine pump. During my surgery, I had lost a lot of blood and had needed transfusions. My new doctor did not like my blood count and ordered two more units of blood. My body reacted and I became bloated, breaking out with huge blisters on my legs and feet. My liver was not accepting the transfusions.

My eyesight went from 20/20 to completely fuzzy overnight, I had a raging fever, and my yellow skin indicated hepatitis. Once again I had no place to turn but to God. But this time I turned to him first. Incredible peace came immediately. Thousands of people were praying for me. I knew the strength of Christ would get me through these latest trials, and I had complete assurance that I was in his care.

My physical battle the next day was no fun at all. The doctor had ordered that I be packed in ice to bring down my raging fever. That was fine for the bottom half of me where I no longer had any sensation. But my chest and upper body could feel the icy water fully. So, for the next several hours, Wendy and my mother enjoyed themselves far too much, dousing me with freezing water and ice cubes. I felt like I was a member of the polar bear club—those guys in Alaska who break through the ice and dive into the frigid water. That night my fever broke, my eyesight came back, new blood tests indicated that my liver was functioning normally, and, thankfully, there was no sign of hepatitis. Do I believe in the power of prayer? You bet I do.

Within a few days, the medical staff deemed me well enough to begin physical therapy. As strange as it may sound, the first stage of my therapy required me to sit up. It had been four weeks since my injury, and I had done nothing but lie flat on my back. I had no idea that sitting up could be such an ordeal, but was it ever. The physical therapists wrapped me in a large abdominal belt to keep my blood pressure stable and put T.E.D. stockings (tight, thick, elastic stockings) on my legs to prevent blood clots.

Gradually, the therapists tilted my specially designed bed a few degrees. Just five degrees made me feel like passing out. I broke out in a cold sweat and became nauseated. Over a couple of days they increased the tilt five more degrees. That continued until I was ready to be placed in a chair. That required a Hoyer lift—quite the experience. If you have ever seen animal rescue shows where they put a cow or horse into a huge sling and raise it up with a helicopter, that is about what it is like.

So there I was, hanging on for dear life, swinging around in a sling while the therapists steered for a chair. If I looked anything like I felt, it must have been quite a show. At last I landed in the chair, slightly reclined, and the nurse said she wanted me to sit up for two hours. Already light-headed and nauseous, the thought of two hours in that position was frightening. But Wendy was with me and kept cold washcloths on my forehead while I sat there with my eyes closed, wishing the world would stop spinning. I lasted for thirty minutes, then started to pass out between episodes of throwing up. Wendy called for help, and the nurse relented. After another "air rescue," wow, was I ever glad to be back in bed. After repeating this ordeal several more times, I was finally able to sit up and stay in a wheelchair.

Now the real fun began—intensive therapy. In the mornings, I swam. Next came physical therapy, lunch, occupational therapy, one last round of physical therapy, and finally bedtime. I learned a lot, and quickly. For example, if a person wants to be loved, they should not become a physical therapist. Mine was about five feet nothing, one hundred pounds, and tough as nails. I remember her name but am afraid to write it down, for fear of what she will do to me if she should ever read this!

In all honesty, my personal physical therapist was worth her weight in gold for the hard work that she invested in me. She even took it in stride when I learned where all of the good hiding places were in the hospital. Using my wheelchair, I could sneak off to the cafeteria at the other end of the hospital or go outside to the break areas. I would even retreat to the main lobby where I tried to blend in with all of the other people in wheelchairs. My therapist and Wendy would search high and low for me. And, of course, they always found me. Then off I went to therapy, grumbling about the "torture chamber."

Now, to those who have never had therapy, it may not sound all that bad. But my therapist would put me (while still in my wheelchair) on a floor mat and insist that I get out of my chair and lie on the floor. "Once you get back into your wheelchair, come and get me," she would say. "I've got some paperwork to do." Then, off she would go to her office.

Sounded like torture to me!

I had a heavy weight to bear, literally. Since my arms now had to do the heavy lifting, lifting weight was necessary to build up my upper body strength. While I grumbled and groaned about my "abuse," it was lighthearted. In truth, I was determined to work hard and to leave the hospital as soon as possible. I wanted to go home so badly I could almost taste the home cooking. Within three weeks, the physical therapy staff was calling me their wonder boy.

I pushed hard to leave the hospital, setting mid-July as my personal goal. Everyone thought that I was unrealistic. They did not know my level of determination. I had to relearn every simple task—bathing, going to the bathroom, dressing, and getting my own drink from the refrigerator. I had to learn to carry a drink to the table without dropping it or splashing it all over myself. Occupational therapy helped me do all of these things and more.

I had to learn how to drive with hand controls instead of using my feet. That was frightening at first, especially to the other passengers in the vehicle with me! Thankfully, we were blessed to find a used van that already had all of the necessary modifications. Learning how to use the modified van took more training and time than I expected. Wendy's prayer life increased a lot in that time, especially when she rode with me. Eventually, both of us got used to the new driving routine.

Part of my occupational therapy was to experience a day out in the real world, to go outside of the confines of the hospital with new limitations. We chose a family outing to a restaurant. There were about ten of us that went "out on the town" that day. It was a beautiful day in June, and it felt wonderful to be away from the hospital, especially to be away from the hospital food.

We found a restaurant not far from the hospital. With Dad pushing my wheelchair, we eagerly filed into the restaurant for good food and fun, and since there were so many of us, we were seated in a large and very nice side room. There were other guests in the room, but they seemed to finish their meals quickly, then left. In no time we had the entire room to ourselves. We thought it was great when the hostess did not bring new guests into the room even though there were empty tables.

We had a wonderful meal and thoroughly enjoyed ourselves as everyone caught me up on what was going on in their lives and at home. As we finished our meal, I was getting tired. It was time to head back to the hospital. Mom offered to push my wheelchair out. Everyone else went before us, and Mom and I brought up the rear, as it were. The borrowed wheelchair was not specifically designed for me. There was a large space between the seat and the back support. As we waited in line to pay, all of a sudden my mother gasped. Everyone around us turned to look. Mom just stood there behind me. "Your pants are down! Your entire backside is showing!" she announced for all to hear. No wonder our area had cleared out so fast so we could have our own personal dining room.

My new life was going to be full of surprises, no doubt. And I had one of two choices in how I reacted to them. I could laugh or I could cry. I chose to laugh. Fifteen years later, I am still laughing! However, both Dad and I have learned how to dress properly before going out.

7

GOING HOME

"To everything there is a season,
and a time to every purpose under the heaven:
A time to be born, and a time to die;
A time to plant,
and a time to pluck up that which is planted;
A time to kill, and a time to heal;
A time to break down, and a time to build up;
A time to weep, and a time to laugh."
(Ecclesiastes 3:1–4)

ver the first one and a half months after my accident, this very familiar Bible passage took on new meaning for me. It reminded me that there was even a time in my life for my accident. I had faced every one of the events in the passage, not over a lifetime, but all in a brief time span. At times I was overwhelmed, but by the grace of God, I came through a stronger man than I had been before my accident. When I finally faced my personal weaknesses, I realized that my only strength was in Jesus Christ. Verses like, "I can do all things through Christ which strengtheneth me," (Philippians 4:13) and, "Some trust in chariots, and some in horses: but we will remember the name of the LORD our God," (Psalm 20:7) became very real to me.

While I had faced the challenges with a fear of the unknown, I was also excited. Now I was going home. I told my doctor on Monday, July 14, that I was checking out on Friday, July 18. He tried to talk me out of it, saying that I still had much to accomplish in therapy before I would be ready to leave. "I guess we should get started immediately then, because I'm leaving on Friday," I countered.

The next four days were filled with efforts to get me ready to leave. When the going-home day finally arrived, I was a bundle of nerves, and I'm sure that I was stressing everyone around me. I answered more questions and signed more forms that day than I can remember. Wendy had wallpapered my hospital room with the hundreds of cards I had received. She took them down and packed them with all of my new medical equipment and wheelchair. Thankfully, my parents were there with their car, too, or there would have been no room for me!

The trip home took about two hours; Wendy drove. The closer we got to home, the quieter I became. Lord, can I handle this? Can I still be a husband and father to my family? My mind raced with apprehension. When we pulled into the driveway, I saw familiar things with a new appreciation—the beautiful pine grove behind our home with its "secret" forts the girls had built, the old-fashioned split rail fence, Rhododendron bushes, count-less varieties of flowers that Wendy had planted around the house, and so much green! When I opened the van door, I breathed in the smell of "pure country." The squeaky weathervane on top of the garage—a noise that had once irritated me—signaled its own personal greet-ing. But quickly I saw other things that overwhelmed me. The yard needed to be mowed, the driveway needed to be swept, and fallen tree branches needed to be picked up. A lot of work demanded my attention.

Appearance had always meant a great deal to me so I was very particular about the way anything looked that involved me—our home, my job performance, even the way we dressed and acted in public. I slowly began to realize that my requirements were not as im-portant as I had always thought. Personal qualities are not inherently bad, but I took them to extremes, and that indicated sinful pride. I blushed when I considered what an arrogant person I had been, thinking I could do everything better than anyone else.

Since the ride had tired me out, it took everyone working together to get me out of the car and into the house so I could lie down. To help me get into the house, a friend had built a ramp. What a help and a great blessing. Inside, we found Kara, Ariel, and Wendy's parents there to greet me. The girls had spent all morning making welcome home posters, hanging balloons, and decorating. They showered me with kisses and hugs. Tears filled my eyes as I soaked in their love.

But new challenges awaited me. The hospital environment had spoiled me. Wide halls, tiled floors, everything was designed to be accessible. Here at home, however, the narrow doors were difficult to navigate, and I had to squeak through carefully to save my fingers. Corners around furniture and walls were difficult to maneuver. The soft carpet felt like pushing my wheelchair through sand. Our step-down dining room, which we once thought was beautiful, was now totally impractical. I barely fit into our very small bathroom. Once inside, I could not turn around, and there was barely enough room to shut the door.

When I squeezed through the door into our bedroom, we realized we would have to move the bed so I could turn my wheelchair enough to transfer. Our antique bed was shorter than standard beds today. Before my injury I had never thought much about the shorter length and just bent my legs a little in order to fit. No longer able to bend my legs, once I got into bed, my head hit the headboard, and my feet hit the footboard. Great, I thought.

While wondering what to do about the bed, a friend showed up to wish me well. We visited for a few minutes in the bedroom, while I put on my best smile for him. As he was leaving, he told me in all sincerity that once my body healed, he was convinced that I would walk again. I knew he meant well, but I also knew he had no idea what I was feeling.

When Wendy came back in to the bedroom after seeing him out, she found me in tears. This homecoming was the first of many days in which discouragement threatened to take over even in the happy times if I would let it. Looking back now, I realize that the trauma of the injury and all of the medication that I was taking wreaked havoc on my emotions. In time, with Wendy's unconditional love, and both of us leaning on the Lord for strength, with diligence and patience, we got through one day at a time.

One by one we made essential changes to the house to make it as accessible as possible without major reconstruction. The kitchen was rearranged so I could reach things without asking for help. My ramp-building friend solved the problem between the kitchen and the dining room.

When my accident happened, Wendy had been employed at a local hospital. When she left the job to be with me, they told her that when she was ready to return, her job would be waiting for her. After a few days at home, Wendy decided to go back to work because she knew that we needed the money. My parents came over frequently so I wouldn't be alone, although I didn't mind fending for myself and even preferred it at times.

To say the least, my first few days at home proved to be difficult. One day, while sitting in the living room alone watching TV, I decided to transfer to the sofa. Pulling next to the sofa for my "leap of faith," I missed and fell between my wheelchair and the sofa. From my training in therapy I knew what to do to get back into my chair. But what had become easy to do on a floor mat in a gym was nearly impossible on the floor in our living room. After several attempts to get back into my wheelchair, I was exhausted and disgusted at myself. In frustration, I gave up.

Taking a pillow from the sofa, I laid back on the floor and watched television from there. Wendy would be home in a couple of hours, and she could help me up. But when she got home and found me on the floor, she decided that staying home with me was more important than money. God always provided, and Wendy is always amazing.

As creatures of habit, we resist change, but sometimes we have to make adjustments. Our family certainly had to change habits and routines to meet new needs. For instance, anyone who has studied geometry knows that the shortest distance between two points is a straight line. That theorem, however, seldom applied in my case. The straight line was not always accessible. One day Wendy and I decided to go to lunch at a small restaurant we liked that was not far from where we lived. But, because it was in an older building, it was not accessible to wheelchairs. So we sought a newer, wheelchair-friendly eating place, and off we went. We found one in a strip mall, with a road separating the store fronts from the parking lot. We parked in a parking spot clearly marked for the disabled, got out of the van, and then realized that even though the restaurant was directly in front of us, the only cutout onto the sidewalk was at the other end of the mall. So, to get from point A to point B, we had to go through point Z. So much for geometry!

We made our little trek and finally went in for lunch. After we ate, there was a line of customers waiting to pay. I told Wendy I would go get in the van and wait for her there. After saying, "Pardon me" several times, squeezing around tables that were very close together, I made it out of the restaurant and onto the sidewalk. There was our van right where we had parked it, twenty-five yards away. But once again, I faced the five-hundred-yard trek to reach the cutout.

In therapy, one of the things I had been taught was how to get on and off sidewalks without cutouts. Being a bit disgusted that there was only one cutout in the entire sidewalk, I decided to practice what I had learned. In the abstract, getting off a sidewalk should be easy—roll up to the edge, pop a wheelie to raise my front wheels up, then roll forward to drop down the five or so inches on my back tires. That would bring my front tires down, and off I would go. But I wasn't in the abstract, I was about to be in the concrete.

Determined to make it work, I rolled up to the edge, waited for a break in traffic, and popped a wheelie. My front wheels lifted up—check—I pushed my wheelchair forward with great care—check—and rolled forward—no check! As my back tires started to roll over the edge, I lost my balance; my front tires dropped down hard; my wheelchair stopped abruptly;

unfortunately, I did not. The forward momentum catapulted me out of the chair, and I went flying onto the middle of the roadway.

As I flew through the air the thought came to me that this was going to hurt, but happily the only thing that got hurt was my pride. As I lay there, my wheelchair somewhere behind me, motorists stopped to block traffic so I wouldn't get hit. Soon I attracted quite a crowd of onlookers. Well-meaning people offered to help, but they had no idea what to do.

Thankfully, I had not been lying there long when Wendy found me. She ran to me, worried that I might be injured, but I wasn't looking for sympathy. "Get me back into my wheelchair so we can get out of here," I whispered. While she helped me, a police car showed up on the scene. Working together, the police officer and Wendy got me into my wheelchair, and I rolled to my van with a red face and a shattered ego. It would never have occurred to me to sue the strip mall; I was just happy I didn't get a ticket for blocking traffic!

Safely in the van, Wendy and I had a good laugh. In fact, we laughed all the way home. So, the shortest distance between two points is a straight line, but for people in wheelchairs, it isn't always the most practical line.

— —

After we were settled in at home, Wendy and I did our best to continue with our lives as usual. Before the accident, we had spent time every summer at the lake house in Shapleigh that belonged to Wendy's parents. We wanted desperately to continue that tradition. But like so many other places, it was not accessible. That was another one of those awakening periods. The accident had not only affected me, it had impacted many others as well.

The church Wendy's parents belong to had planned a cookout and work day at the lake for the last Saturday in July. We planned to attend. But, when we arrived at the lake house, I looked at the steps and realized that there was no way I could get inside. Within minutes our neighbors came over to say hello. And without hesitation, they lifted me and my wheelchair up the steps and through the front door.

Over the next hour, at least one hundred people arrived from the church. They came with their trucks loaded down with building supplies and equipment. They fired up their grills, and soon the wonderful smell of barbeque filled the air. They had brought in enough food for an army. They designed and built a large ramp, widened doors, and converted a downstairs room into a beautiful bedroom.

Neighbors that I barely knew and who had never been a part of my life became good friends. My parents' church building is over two hundred years old and had never had a need for accessibility. They, too, installed a ramp, widened doors, and even added a wheelchair-accessible bathroom.

Wendy and I had a favorite restaurant on the beach that we loved to visit during our summers in Maine. When the owner saw me in my wheelchair, she commissioned the city council to bypass months of red tape in order to build a fantastic ramp so that I could enter.

I could never list all of the kindnesses shown to me and my family.

In fifteen years God has continued to bring wonderful people into our lives who continue to help us in amazing ways. By God's grace, I hope to continue to do things that will have a positive Christ-centered impact on them. But I am truly the one that is most blessed.

8

911

While "difficult" can hardly begin to describe my time in the hospital, Wendy and I recognized that the real challenge lay before us—our day-to-day survival. As we pieced our lives back together one project at a time, our daughters were so full of life and energy that I had little time to whine or complain. Still, there were days when I wanted to do nothing but grumble about my new lot in life.

Everything that I did took extra time and effort. Personal grooming and preparation for the day that took thirty minutes in my previous life, now took two hours. Short errands—like running to gas up the van or picking up a package at the post office—were now out of the question. Since it took me at least ten minutes to get in my van and another ten to get out, I thought long and hard about which trips were worth the effort; often Wendy had to do them.

In fact, there were many things that I could no longer do at all. In our backyard we had several bird feeders. I had enjoyed my job of keeping them filled. But, even if I worked out a way to manage the bags of birdseed stored in the garage, I could not climb a step ladder to refill the feeders. Like most homes in the north, ours had a full basement, which was now off limits to me. As a result, I had to leave things at the top of the stairway for others to take downstairs, or post a list of things for them to bring back up to me.

High cupboards and shelves that were out of reach required a "reacher" for me to grab things beyond my grasp. A reacher looks like a pair of salad tongs on the end of a pole. It has a handle to squeeze that closes the rubber-tipped gripping device—the "tongs." It worked well on lightweight items, but opening cabinet doors was a problem, and I often dropped heavier items. My use of the reacher created more work for Wendy, but she put it to good use in her own tasks. It was great for retrieving pesky socks that fell behind the dryer. So we think every home should have one!

When family and friends came to visit, they often didn't know what to say to me and sometimes avoided coming at all. But, as always, my family remained faithful. The Lord gave me grace as my grumbling days became fewer and my good days increased. I, too, needed to be faithful.

Many people that I had once looked upon as friends slowly drifted away. Who could blame them? I was a different person. I had been extremely active, constantly on the go, had one project after another going at all times, and was involved in too many organizations. Psalm 46:10 says, "Be still, and know that I am God." God was gently blowing away the chaff in my life and was using my injury to reset my priorities, purging and purifying my heart. I had to let go of relationships and activities that were no longer needed to satisfy my ambitions.

The accident slowed down the pace of my life. My life had been about "doing," and I rarely took time to sit back and enjoy life itself. My high school history teacher had told me, "Silence is golden; listen to it." Practicing that precious truth, I listened to others—my girls, my wife, my family, and my good friends. What I heard were words of love and encouragement.

As the New England summer transitions to fall, there are many things to do to prepare for the long Maine winters. Unable to do many of those things without asking others for help, routine tasks brought regular opportunities to learn humility.

Wendy and I tackled these jobs with our focus on what I could do, rather than on what I could not do. We had a push mower, so Wendy took over mowing. Raking leaves became her responsibility, too. My job was to run the leaf blower. I sat in the driveway in my wheelchair and blew the leaves into piles, making them easier to pick up. With bush cutters in hand, I trimmed the shrubs as far as I could reach, and Wendy topped them off.

Dad was an incredible help, often showing up to rescue Wendy. When he and Mom popped in for a visit, Dad instantly jumped in and went to work. He saw things that needed to be done and did them without being asked. It saddened me to sit by watching my dad prune our trees, winterize our house, and take care of the many responsibilities that were once my jobs.

When Wendy was not physically able to help me, I called my dad. A quick phone call to my parents and they were on their way. One time, when I was regaining my strength, I was in the bathtub and could not get out. Wendy could not lift me, so she called my parents. They immediately headed out on the forty-five-minute drive while I sat in the tub waiting to be rescued. When Mom and Dad arrived, the ladies visited together in the living room, rocking away and talking, while Dad struggled to hoist me out of the tub. Yes, I was embarrassed, but Dad never was. He would do anything to help me or Wendy—shovel snow, change light bulbs, hoist a water-logged son out of the bathtub—anything. They helped whenever they could. My brothers have the same servants' hearts. I have never doubted that any of them would help whenever and however they could.

Coming to the point of asking for help was difficult for me. It was hard to sit back and let others do for me what I wanted so badly to do for myself. A good friend who saw me hesitate told me in a few short words exactly what I needed to hear. "Rick," Tim spoke in all seriousness, "don't deny others the blessing of serving."

I had not considered my new circumstances from any viewpoint but my own until that moment—it was my pride rearing its ugly head again. Tim was right, and he got me thinking. This was not a new concept, just one I hadn't embraced. When pride tells us we should have it our way, it affects all areas of our lives.

Thinking it was a virtue, I was extremely particular about how things should be done, while Wendy has never been as picky as I was. I surprised myself, and I'm sure I surprised Wendy, when I saw that it didn't matter when the lawn was not manicured flawlessly or the shrubs trimmed to perfection, or even that the rake skipped over a leaf here and there. We agreed that if the bed didn't get made every day, life would still go on. If a piece of furniture was not placed just so in the room because I needed space to navigate, the furniture-placement police would not show up at the front door with an arrest warrant. Others confined to wheelchairs know what I'm talking about. I had not realized how silly I behaved over such inconsequential things.

Shortly after my injury, when winter arrived, bringing with it our first big snowstorm of the season, it snowed throughout the day with no signs of it letting up. As we got ready for bed, I kept looking out at our driveway, worried sick that the fluffy white stuff was piling up and needed to be shoveled out quickly. One by one, we all settled down for "our long winter's nap." But sleep wouldn't come to me because I was worried about "doing." Eventually, I shut my eyes and was able to doze off.

I slept restlessly for a few hours. Then suddenly something awakened me. I glanced at the clock and saw that it was 4:00 a.m. Suddenly I heard a loud bang outside. Listening intently, I heard more loud bangs and other noises I could not identify.

Loving husband that I am, I woke Wendy and asked her if she had heard anything. She moaned incomprehensibly, then drifted back to sleep. It was quiet for a few minutes, and then I heard more commotion. I tapped Wendy. "It sounds like someone is trying to break into the store down the road. Go look out the window and see what's going on."

Wendy pretty much told me I was nuts and to go back to sleep. I lay there for about five more minutes listening to the distant banging noises until I couldn't take it any longer. "If she is not going to deal with this, I'm calling the police," I thought. I picked up the phone and punched 9-1-1. Finally, Wendy came around enough to realize what I had done and agreed to check it out before I did something foolish. I had already hit the last digit, but I hurriedly hung up the phone before my call could register and anyone had time to answer—or so I thought.

We lived in a small town where everyone knew Wendy, me, our families, and my new circumstances. The whole community was alert to our needs. Wendy assured me that I was imagining things as she threw back the covers. As she dragged herself out of bed, the phone and the doorbell rang simultaneously. I answered the phone. It was the police department following up on my disconnected 911 call. Wendy gave me a look that could have withered an oak tree as she stormed out of the bedroom. Opening the front door, she found herself face-to-face with a police officer.

"I'm going to kill him," I heard Wendy's voice coming from down the hallway.

After being greeted in that manner, the officer asked to come in to look around (or maybe to make sure that she didn't follow through on her threat).

"Come in." Her tone was not exactly welcoming.

Even though the police officer knew who we were, he remained professional. "Dispatch received a 911 disconnect call from this residence," he explained. "I need to check out the premises to make sure everything is okay."

Wendy explained to the officer what had happened—new injury, recently home from the hospital, hearing things . . . " Flipping on the lights, she escorted the policeman from room to room.

As they approached the girls' bedroom, just down the hall from ours, I heard Wendy whisper to the officer, "Try not to wake up the girls."

They proceeded down the hall to our bedroom. The policeman entered and shined his flashlight in my face. There I was, blankets pulled up to my chin, looking like a very guilty little boy. I confessed my crime and told him I was terribly sorry.

"The noise you heard was the snowplow down the road, scraping snow off the store parking lot," the officer explained.

No one was laughing at that moment, but when we remember that night or tell this story to others, Wendy and I laugh ourselves silly to this day. Wait till you hear the "rest of the story."

Earlier that night, Wendy had decided to apply a deep-conditioning beauty treatment to her hair—sort of a home remedy. Right before going to bed, she slathered almost an entire jar of mayonnaise through her hair. From my vantage point as I watched the officer point his light in every nook and cranny of the room, I caught a hint of humor in his eyes. While it may have been his reaction to my foolishness—no doubt that would be Wendy's point of view—I'm more inclined to believe that his not-so-subtle grin was a response to the "mayo paste" causing my wife's hair to stick out in every direction!

Wendy usually has a sweet and mild demeanor, but even she has her limit. Apparently, waking her up in the middle of the night to host an open house for a local police officer could upset even Wendy. So, men, if you plan to call 911 and hang up or to bravely send your wife to the door at 4:00 a.m., tell her to "hold the mayo!"

When morning came, Wendy bundled up to go out and attack the foot of new snow on our driveway. As I watched out the window, fighting against the icy wind and shoveling the heavy snow, I loved her, but as a man, I felt useless. It seemed no matter what she did for me, my male ego drove me to focus on myself. But I knew that focusing on my frustration was selfish. I needed to pick up the slack where I could. Going into the kitchen, I found the coffee, placed a filter in the pot, and started brewing coffee. When Wendy came inside to warm up for a few minutes, the aroma of fresh coffee greeted her. She was so excited that I had thought enough about her to offer such a simple act of kindness. She still talks about how much that single act of love meant to her. I had so much yet to learn, but I was beginning to understand that I could still make a difference in people's lives, often in ways I once considered too insignificant to matter.

Oh, and as a side note, you need to know what a true romantic I am. That year for Valentine's Day, I bought Wendy a snow blower! Too bad I didn't think to tell her how nice her hair looked.

9

THE MIGHTY HUNTER

In 2002, the Wounded Warrior Project (WWP) was founded in Roanoke, Virginia. Organized to help injured veterans returning from war to get acclimated back into civilian life, this program hosts events for disabled veterans, often partnering with other organizations. One such event is deer hunting, which is open for disabled veterans and any individuals in wheelchairs that wish to participate. Because I loved hunting when growing up, I was excited to find a way to enjoy it again. I look forward to these hunts each year. They offer me many opportunities to share my own experience with others and tell them how God has sustained me through every trial. They also remind me that I can choose to laugh or I can choose to cry.

Very early on an October Saturday morning, I got up to prepare for my first deer hunt of the year. Through the perfect autumn day I drove to the agreed location to meet the other hunters. Because I really love these events, I want everything to be perfect before I go, so once I get there I can enjoy hanging out with the guys.

When I arrived, I parked on a nice, flat cement surface to make it easy to get out of my van, even though it was a little bit out of the way. But, when I got out, the van door would not close behind me. I decided that was no big deal. This wasn't the first time that had happened. For some reason, the timing on my automatic door gets out of sync, but with a little manual effort on my part, it is relatively easy to fix. I played around with it for a couple of minutes, thinking I could have it working in no time. But this time my efforts were to no avail. (What to do?)

I had two options. I could find someone to manually fold in the ramp and shut the door for me, or I could attempt to do it myself. So, being the big "Macho Man," I decided on the second option. As I lifted the ramp up to fold it in, the top half started to fold back down, flipping me and my wheelchair over backward. I lay on the cement upside down as the lift slowly settled back down on top of me. (Nice.)

The first thing I did, of course, was to quickly look around to see if anyone was noticing me flopping around like a fish out of water. Nope, all was good. Thinking, I've got this, I dragged myself and my wheelchair out from under the ramp—no easy task on cement. But, as I did so, I realized that my pants and underwear were not coming with me. (Potential embarrassment here.) Every few inches, I stopped to hike up my britches and make sure that everything was dragging with me. At last, I got out from under the ramp and sat up to assess the damages and then try to figure out how to get back into my wheelchair. Sitting on cold cement is not the best thing for a paraplegic to do, so I grabbed my wheelchair cushion to sit on while I pondered the situation. Glancing around, I saw that I still had not been noticed. The possibility of yelling for help was beginning to look better and better.

My physical therapist had told me that I should be able to get myself back into my wheelchair from the ground with no problem. Yeah, right! When I was twenty years younger and thirty pounds lighter! Where was she when I needed her? There I sat. At last two hunting guides noticed me as they were walking to their big macho 4 x 4 pickup truck. I motioned to them, and they came running. When Wendy's sister heard about this, she made a loving comment as only a sister-in-law could make: "Oh, please tell me that you had to yell, 'YOO-HOO'!"

I did not yell yoo-hoo, but even so, I knew that at that moment I was not "the man." They deftly picked me up and put me back in my chair. Thanking them profusely, I slowly rolled away.

At last I made it to the barn to join the rest of the hunters and quickly disappeared into the crowd. We had a good lunch, and I visited with friends that I had not seen in a while. Our host led the way, and we drove to his property where we would be hunting for the next two days on four hundred acres of beautiful wooded land. It was great to be out of suburbia for a while. After receiving some nice gifts provided by the Department of Natural Resources, we split up. Jim, the other disabled hunter in our group, was taken to his deer-hunting blind, and I was taken to mine. The blinds were small lean-tos on the ground, constructed with wooden floors so that we could roll our wheelchairs in with little effort.

Mine looked rickety, but surely it would hold up at least for the day. In I rolled, while my guide helped me set things up. "All set?" he asked. I assured him I was, so he drove my van away, leaving me alone for the afternoon and evening. As I watched him disappear over the last hill, I backed up my wheelchair to improve my view, and my left back wheel crashed through the floor of the stand!

I was in danger of going over backward again, knowing if I did, the entire stand would go with me. I tried to roll out of the hole in the floor, but my wheels merely spun. The rotted floor continued to break open. This was not only embarrassing, it was dangerous. There I sat, my front wheels about six inches in the air, leaning my torso as far forward as I could so I wouldn't tip over backward. Great, I thought. My only choice was to use the walkie-talkies that we had been given in case we needed to call for help. Of course, everyone with a walkie-talkie would hear me. I couldn't believe that after only five minutes into the hunt, I was forced to call for help. I pressed the little squawk button and quietly spoke my name to see if anyone could hear me. One of our guides answered back, and I explained the situation as briefly as possible. "On my way," he assured me.

In about five minutes, my rescuer pulled up in a four-wheeler. He helped me out of the broken floor, and I moved to the front side of the blind where the floor was stable. He apologized over and over, and I assured him it was no problem. He drove away, and I got myself situated again. "This is ridiculous," I chuckled and was very glad to be alone so no one could see me crack up laughing at myself. Finally I settled down and, like any good hunter, sat very still and didn't make another sound.

Two gray squirrels chased each other in the trees nearby. I didn't think I would see anything else, considering how my day had begun. But the day ended well. I shot two nice-sized does. When the guide came back, he picked up the deer and took us to the processing station to have my venison packed and frozen. I was bringing home some fresh venison, so I felt better about the entire day.

This tale of the mighty hunter reminds us that we all need a good laugh now and then at our own expense—it helps to keep us humble. But, there is more to it than that. There is nothing inherently unique about human problems, or how we react to them. All people, disabled or otherwise, face daily challenges. The way we handle those challenges exposes our view of the working of God in our lives. In 1 Corinthians 10:13 we read, "There hath no temptation taken you but such as is common to man; but God is faithful, who will not suffer you to be tempted above that ye are able; but will with the temptation also make a way to escape, that ye may be able to bear it."

After I was helped back into my wheelchair, I could have chosen to leave the hunt in disgust. Then I could have skipped the next hunt, then the grocery store, then Walmart, and before I knew it, I could have chosen never to leave my home again. Sadly, I know many people who have responded that way. Instead of relying on God's daily grace, they choose to retreat, hiding from the world, angry at God for what they perceive is a unique injustice inflicted upon them. In my case, I have been learning to look for the lesson that God is unfolding for me, and by God's grace, I hope to continue to do so.

10

WITH WINGS AS EAGLES

Because I want to be an encouragement to others, I have written about my injury, illustrated by stories about my life in a wheelchair. I want to tell others that people can live with disabilities and that life doesn't have to be over. The world continues to turn, winter changes to spring, and spring ushers in summer. We can wallow in self-pity or choose to live and give glory to God. Personally, I have never looked at my wheelchair as an injustice or some evil punishment from God. My wheelchair shows me on a daily basis that God loves me. He could have left me mired in the sinful ways of the world. If it took a wheelchair for me to have a close relationship with my heavenly Father, then I would choose it all again.

One year after the accident, Wendy and I agreed that I should go back to school. My time in rehab made me realize that many people who had undergone injuries similar to mine had tremendous difficulties coping. In many cases the hurting individual did not have the support system of a strong family or a personal relationship with Jesus Christ to see them through. Wendy and I were asked many questions. Most questions had very little to do with the physical injury. On the contrary, people were searching for emotional and spiritual answers. When hurting people ask the question "why," they are not looking for some technical answer. They are asking the gut-wrenching question of how to find hope in a world turned upside down.

When people saw that Wendy and I had a strength that many others did not, we were thrust into a ministry of helping others cope with their injuries and fears.

As opportunities came, we shared our faith. We often prayed with families and opened God's Word, where hope is found. What a joy it has been to see hopelessness turn to confident faith in the power of Jesus Christ.

So that I could further my education, Wendy, Kara, Ariel, and I packed up and headed to Bob Jones University in Greenville, South Carolina, where I planned to earn a degree in biblical counseling. I had survived a traumatic injury, and my life had changed, but the process of growth was not over. There was still a lot to learn and a lot of life to experience. I could not sit at home in my wheelchair and let it pass me by.

In 2003, I earned my Bachelor of Arts in biblical counseling. College took on a meaning for me that it had not held the first time around. I did not pursue the degree in order to chase the empty dreams of fame and fortune, as I had before. My new purpose was to equip myself with the proper tools so that I could serve God by ministering to people that were hurting. Instead of studying failed psychological models, my counseling classes taught me how to help people using God's Word. The Bible classes were priceless! I read, studied, learned, and used every lesson by first applying it to my own life. In addition, my studies prepared me for the increasing opportunities of ministry. Those opportunities to serve and to help others have opened up not only for me but for my entire family. Wendy, Kara, and Ariel are an integral part of everything we do. They all have such tender spirits for the things of God.

The Lord has brought volunteer activities in which I can serve other people with disabilities, such as starting peer support groups, working for a spinal cord injury association, serving on a state disabilities commission, doing inspirational speaking at schools and community centers, and participating in wheelchair sports teams. Best of all, I have been able to share my faith in Christ with others in churches around the country. Many people think that being in full-time ministry means being a pastor, evangelist, missionary, or Christian school teacher. I am none of the above, but I know that God has brought people into my life that needed salvation or the hope that only God's Word can offer during a crisis. Ministry opportunities occur whenever we serve with a willing heart.

I once received a phone call from an organization here in South Carolina that asked me to make a home visit to a person in a wheelchair. A friend of mine, also in a wheelchair, made the visit with me. As we drove to the address, I wondered about our safety because of the surrounding neighborhood.

We arrived at an apartment building that should have been condemned and torn down. As we found the right number and knocked on the door, I noticed bullet holes in the windows. Someone inside yelled over the blare of a television for us to come in. When we rolled in, we found ourselves in a small room of bare cinderblock. It had cement floors, and old discarded pieces of furniture were spread around. We were greeted by a man in a wheelchair who wore only an undershirt and an adult diaper. I introduced us and told him I had been called to check on him to see how he was doing. We could already tell how he was doing, but I had to start somewhere.

The place was filthy beyond imagination, and the stench was almost unbearable. Lord, help me with what to do here, I prayed. We stayed for about thirty minutes and got information from him concerning his case, names of social workers, and any groups that he was in touch with for assistance. Before we left, we prayed with him, and I left one of my tracts for him to read.

Back at home, I made several phone calls on his behalf. Serving on the Commission for the Department of Disabilities and Special Needs at the time, I knew the right people to contact. The Head and Spinal Cord Injury division took immediate action to help the man. Within a week he was in a decent apartment, receiving the care that he desperately needed. Granted, this was an extreme way to give a gospel tract, but it was the Christ-like thing to do. The gentleman was grateful that someone cared enough to help, and his spirits were lifted when we left as he held the gospel in his hand.

I have handed out many gospel tracts to some who have later called me and thanked me for caring. I have ministered to people whose bodies have been eaten up with cancer. I have had the joy of praying with them, bringing peace and comfort, often within hours before they passed into glory. I have waited patiently in emergency rooms with families as their loved one's future hinged on life or death from an accident. I have watched the tears of family members as they settled their own relationship with Jesus Christ. I have shared my testimony in churches and seen hands raised during the invitation indicating the need of salvation or of God's peace that passes all understanding.

Yes, I have laughed with people, cried with people, and prayed with people. Once, I had the privilege of going on a mission trip with a co-worker in Christ. We spoke as a team at several churches, sharing our testimonies and how God has been faithful in our lives, even though both of us are in wheelchairs. Although life is filled with trials and many people lose hope and want to give up, when two men in wheelchairs share how wonderful God is and how blessed and thankful we are for being in a wheelchair, people listen.

Each year Wendy opens our home for a Christmas party. We invite all of the people that we know with disabilities who are in our peer support group. We have a great turnout and have had as many as fifteen people in wheelchairs in our home. (You need traffic control when you have that many wheels in one house.) We have a great meal, sing Christmas carols, hand out gifts, and share testimonies. Kara and Ariel help with these events by assisting people in and out of vehicles, offering valet parking, contributing music specials, serving food, and sometimes sitting with children so their parents could come. It has been such a joy for Wendy and me to see our daughters so willing to serve as we watch them work with disabled individuals.

Some people look at faith as nothing more than a crutch. Let me assure you it is not that at all. There is an old morality play, *Everyman*, in which a man that has everything in life gets ill and is facing death. As he gets closer and closer to his final days, he is deserted by his false friends and family. He loses his wealth, his wits, his strength, and everything else that he has valued in this life. In the end, he comes to realize that he can take nothing he has received from this life into eternity, but only what he has given in service to God.

Remembering the early days of trials and tears, albeit with much laughter, I don't see how I ever thought I could have made it through life on my own. My faith changed and grew to something that can never be taken away. An accident robbed me of the use of two-thirds of my body, but my personal relationship with Jesus restored my soul. This is not a sob story about my broken body, it is my sincere attempt to give God the glory for breaking my stubborn will. It is the best thing that ever happened to me.

APPENDIXES

Wendy when she was sixteen, the year Rick and she met; Rochester, New Hampshire, 1980

From left to right: Bruce, Rick & Steve Huntress; Shapleigh, Maine, 1988

Wendy's parents, Wendell and Hilda Clough; Wells
Beach, Maine, 2010

Wendy (above) and Rick (below) with parents Charlie
and Joan Huntress; Wells Beach, Maine, 2011

Rick in uniform holding Kara; Charlotte, North Carolina, 1990

Picture drawn by six-year-old Ariel the night she learned of her dad's injury; May 14, 1997

5/97

will you Be
paralyzed? because

I do not want you
paralyzed. did you
you no that I
Love you Kang does Love
to. When you are home
will you play
With me if you
Can? how are you
doing? we are doing fine

Rick H.
Ariel H. — age 6

Letter that Ariel wrote to Rick after learning of his accident; 1997

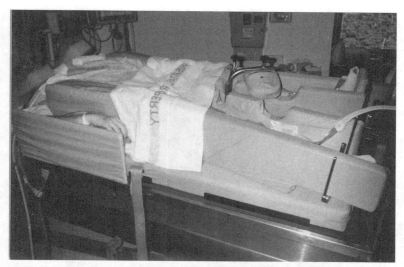

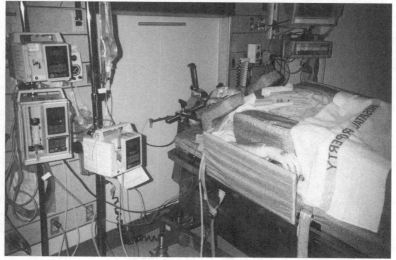

Rick in Stryker bed, ICU; 1997

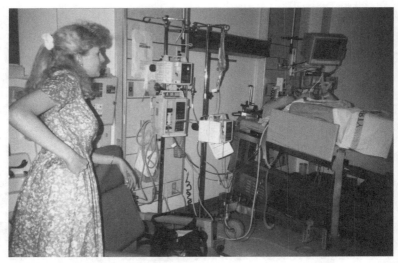

Wendy & Rick in ICU; 1997

Eisenhower Medical Center at Fort Gordon, Georgia
where Rick had his surgery; 1997

One year after the accident; 1998

Back row left to right: Kara, Wendy, Ariel and Rick on recumbent bike starting out on walk-a-thon raising money for the Multiple Sclerosis Foundation; Greenville, South Carolina, 2003

Rick's graduation from Bob Jones University; 2003

Back row left to right: Ariel, Kara, Wendy, and Rick at Ein Gedi, Israel, Tour for Disabled; 2010

WE CAN STILL DREAM

Following my accident I figured I would have to give up on many of my dreams. As the years progressed, I realized that my injury had not stopped me from living. During Christmas vacation of 2010 one very special dream came true—my long-held desire to take a trip to Israel.

Working closely with Shalom Ministries, I helped plan a trip for disabled travelers. Much discussion ensued concerning every aspect of the trip—hotel reservations, bus accommodations, site accessibility, and how many able-bodied people would be needed to make all of this work. The plans resulted in seven of us, along with friends and family, experiencing the trip of a lifetime.

Mount Carmel

What an amazing adventure! We met the challenge head on, but not without much huffing and puffing from our able bodied assistants.

Our bus driver was great and brought us right to the entrance of the park area. The parking lot was manageable, but the paving stones were rough and jagged. The front wheels on our wheelchairs constantly got caught in the large cracks between the stones. I would pop a wheelie and move ahead about six inches. Then I would pop another wheelie and move ahead again. It was uphill from the parking lot to our destination, which was the main building with a rooftop lookout. Our friends and family helped. Since I have use of my upper body, I made slow but steady progress. Wendy and my daughters, not far away, were helping others. When we first entered the building we found ourselves in a gift shop with a flat floor. Nice! Something those of us who travel on wheels never take for granted.

And now the real fun began. Our leader was determined that all of us would get to the lookout on the roof of the building, so that we could see the vast landscape before us. The only "minor" thing standing between us and our destination was two large flights of stairs. After looking the situation over, our leader announced, "Here we go!" He and his son picked up and carried one of us to the top, while my daughter carried the man's wheelchair for him. This particular man didn't weigh much so that worked out pretty well. One by one, with lots of help and rest stops along the way, each man was carried to the rooftop.

I was the last to go. I am not a small man and my leader humorously suggested I consider going on a diet. I backed up to the stairs and then with him holding and lifting the handles on my wheelchair, and others holding and lifting the front of my wheelchair, we began the climb one step at a time. Up. Rest. Up. Rest. Up. Rest. The goal was to keep my wheelchair level so I would stay in my chair and not perform a nose-dive down the stairs. At that time I weighed one-hundred-ninety pounds, and my wheelchair weighed about thirty-five pounds. After a much-needed quick rest on the landing, we started on flight number two. Both of my daughters are used to dealing with situations such as this. Stairs are an inevitable part of life. But this was all new to our helpers. Like many to come, they handled this situation with laughter and determination. But we were relieved once we all made it to the flat, smooth surface of the rooftop.

The view overlooking the Plain of Sharon, the Jezreel Valley, and the Mediterranean Sea was incredible. Mount Carmel ("the Vineyard of God") is the location that Elijah chose to demonstrate the power of God against the false god Baal and his prophets. Elijah knew that from this vantage point, the fire and smoke would be seen for many miles. Looking across the valleys that spread before us, we couldn't help but be moved. We were gazing at the very location where the Bible tells us the final battle of the ages will take place.

Whether in a wheelchair or not, going down stairs is always easier than going up. With much laughter we all made it to the bottom. The wonder of everything we had just witnessed was fresh on our hearts. And with us, too, was the knowledge that for the remainder of our trip, we could do anything!

The Sea of Galilee

One of the most exciting speaking opportunities I have had since my accident took place in a boat on the Sea of Galilee. Our group toured the "Jesus Boat" museum at Nof Ginosar. Because the rain had turned into a light mist at this point, we decided to walk/roll a short distance to our next stop for a boat ride. From the museum we crossed over to a downhill paved sidewalk that brought us to the boat launch. We had been eager to get out onto the water—until we saw how it had to be done. Suddenly the journey up and down two flights of stairs at Mr. Carmel looked easy.

The deck of the boat was free of any structures or obstacles, so that wasn't a problem. The challenge was getting five wheelchairs onto the boat in the first place. If not for the detailed planning of our tour leader months in advance, this boat excursion would not have been possible. Because our leader had prearranged the boarding, four men ran from the boat to our group all ready to push, pull, lift, and do whatever it would take to make it happen.

The first part of the very long dock passage to the boat was a ramp made from corrugated steel. To get onto this first ramp there was about an eight-inch curb to deal with. The rainy weather didn't help the situation. I pulled up to the ramp and popped a wheelie to get my front wheels onto the ramp. One of the four men helping stood behind me holding the handles on my wheelchair, and one of them was in front of me holding the front of my wheelchair. The ramp was not level but more like an inverted V.

While all of this was going on, I explained to our helpers the best way to assist us. They were not used to dealing with people in wheelchairs, but their willingness more than made up for their lack of experience. With my front wheels on the ramp, I told the guy behind me to lift my handles and push me onto the ramp. Neither the incline nor decline of the ramp was extreme, but the rain had made the steel very slippery. The guy pulling in front could get no traction, I could get no traction, and the guy behind me could get no traction. I grabbed the railings on the ramp to pull myself along while the two helpers pushed and pulled. Then we hit the decline side of the ramp and things became interesting. The weight of me and my wheelchair, in addition to the traction problem, started the three of us sliding down the other side. We stopped and turned my wheelchair around backwards to go down the ramp. There was less chance that I would take a nose dive, and I could hold onto the railings better to help. Then the other two assistants jumped in to help, and we slowly moved down the ramp. They lifted me down three steps on the other side onto a flat dock section. I rolled as far as I could and then stopped and waited for the others to follow.

Finally we all passed the first point of our obstacle course. We were lifted onto a second ramp with a slight decline to the next dock section. From there we were lifted a third time onto a downhill ramp, and then hoisted to the final dock section where the boat was moored. Because of the weather, the water was very choppy, and the boat was rocking at a pretty steep pitch. I instantly thought of Peter walking on the water. I liked that thought since I was to give a biblical challenge once we were out on the water.

As if the difficulty of getting to the boat wasn't enough, it was now necessary to get the five of us in wheelchairs lifted about three feet off the dock, up and over the side of a rocking boat, and down three steps onto the deck of the boat! The four men helping never gave it a second thought. Using two large Styrofoam squares as a makeshift stairway, they got us up to the side of the boat. They lifted each of us to the first step, then the second, then over the side of the boat, down the three steps and onto the deck. SAFE!

Sitting in a boat on the Sea of Galilee made the small trial of getting there worth it all. We no sooner got out onto the sea when the rain stopped, the wind stopped, and calmness settled across the water. The Lord performed another miracle that day, and I was so blessed to be a part of it. To survey the scene before me and to realize that so much of Christ's ministry happened right here—so many miracles, so much teaching—was beyond my expectations. I was held in complete awe of the beauty and the sense of biblical history surrounding me. I had the double blessing of sharing a devotional with our group while out on the water. I took my text from Matthew 14 and the fact that Peter went under when he took his eyes off of God. I was reminded that the same thing happens to each of us when we take our eyes off of our heavenly Father.

Adding to our pleasure, the boat owners—who were extremely talented in music—entertained us with wonderful Israeli folk music and English hymns. The memories I hold from my time on the Sea of Galilee are still strong in my mind. For anyone with a disability, let this be an encouragement to never give up. Never say it cannot be done.

Overlooking the Mediterranean Sea at Caesarea, Israel: Tadd Hamblen, Clare Baughman, Terry Washer and Rick

Prearranged assistants helping Rick onto the boat on the Sea of Galilee, Tour for Disabled; 2010

Rick giving a devotional on the boat; Sea of Galilee

Rick overlooking the Jezreel Valley in Israel. He was carried to the top of Mt. Carmel for this amazing view; 2010

Rick at the Temple Mount; Jerusalem, Israel; 2010

TESTIMONY AND POEM
by Joyce Folsom Johnson

You might say that I have known Rick Huntress since before he was born. I remember his grandparents, Carl and Carlotta Huntress. I have known his father and mother, Charles and Joan Huntress, since we were young. I watched Rick grow up. My family and I used to sit in the pew behind Charles, Joan, Rick, and his two brothers at the First Baptist Church in Shapleigh, Maine. Because of this, I was devastated to receive the phone call that Rick had been critically injured in the accident that would confine him to a wheelchair for the rest of his life.

The first time that I saw Rick after his accident, he was sitting in his wheelchair at the front of the church with his wife and two daughters. I was overwhelmed with the emotion of how he must be feeling now that he would be confined to a wheelchair. Then the Lord began giving me the following poem. I jotted it down on the bulletin and gave to Rick at the end of the service.

RICK HUNTRESS

Thank You, dear Lord, for saving my life.
Thank You for my two children and wife.
Thank You for all of my loved ones who pray
Thank You for their support every day.

Thank You for these two strong arms I can use.
Thank You for all that I did not lose
Thank You that I can still hold those I love.
Thank You for holding me from above.

BROKEN AT LAST

by Ariel Huntress
"To Dad"

Because a falsehood entangled our brains,
My young family faced trials and pains,
But my family, fueled by fun and fancy,
Is now different, some would even say crazy.

First of all, this is being told
By someone who was not very old.
I was seven when this confusion mocked my mind,
But my God was merciful, healing, and kind.

Once a young man forgot a necessity
That God is in charge of him and his family.
He ruled his family in a way that is good,
But let me remind you, it was forgetting our God.

God had mercy on our apathetic blindness
And forced, through pain, our souls to confess.
For this young man was instantly paralyzed,
Our family was broken and newly traumatized.
But as many men have beforehand stated,

That of everything here that God has created,
The things that need or are willing to be broken
Are the only things that can become God's useable token.
Take, for instance, an egg and a shell,

It must be breakable or it will not sell.
As the shell shatters, so our life was in pieces,
And even nine years later our testimony increases.
And now our family is happy and free

To love each other, but more importantly
To love our God, serve him together,
And stick to him hard, as a bird and its feather.

EPILOGUE

The young woman stood in the hospital doorway looking at her now-disabled husband. "I want a divorce," she said. "We had so many plans—traveling, building a home, children—and now all of that is gone. I did not sign up for this, and I still need to live my life."

The young man, wounded in body and spirit, turned his head to stare out the window. A tear rolled down his cheek as he struggled with the thought that he must somehow make her understand. He turned his face back to the door with a plea for help on his lips, but she was gone.

Something out of a movie? No. A story that Wendy and I have heard all too often. All of the counseling degrees in the world could not give them hope. Not all people who are injured, disabled, or diagnosed with a debilitating disease have someone like Wendy in their lives offering unconditional love. So, how do I offer these people hope? I do it by directing them to the only hope for any of us—the confident expectation that Jesus Christ will never leave us nor forsake us. Hope relies on that personal relationship with him above all else.

Recently, Wendy and I have had the joy of seeing a couple restored who had been separated. Wendy was able to have many talks with the wife, and I was able to minister to the husband personally and through a Bible study. Through marriage counseling with their pastor, and I hope through Wendy and me, they have a renewed hope in their marriage. It came about because of a restored and personal relationship with Jesus Christ.

No relationship of this world will ever be perfect—not marriage, not children, not parents, not friends. If you are basing your hope and personal happiness on anyone other than Jesus Christ, you will be disappointed. Settle your own relationship with him first, and then you will be filled with the hope that can never be taken away.

"But they that wait upon the LORD shall renew their strength; they shall mount up with wings as eagles; they shall run, and not be weary; and they shall walk, and not faint" (Isaiah 40:31).

Life still has so much to offer. With God's help, perhaps I still have much to offer, too. Quitting is not an option. Laugh every chance you get, cry when you need to, but most of all, make sure that your eternal destiny is a settled matter with God's only Son, Jesus Christ.